Panels & Patchwork

Fast-Finish Panel Projects
for kids on the go!

LANDAUER BOOKS

Panels & Patchwork™
Fast-Finish Panel Projects
for kids on the go!

This book was designed, produced, and published by Landauer Books
A division of Landauer Corporation
3100 NW 101st Street, Urbandale, IA 50322
800-557-2144   www.landauercorp.com

President/Publisher: Jeramy Lanigan Landauer
Director of Operations: Kitty Jacobson
Editor in Chief: Becky Johnston
Managing Editor: Jeri Simon
Art Director: Laurel Albright
Project Designer: Janet Wecker-Frisch
Technical Writer: Rhonda Matus
Editorial Assistant: Debby Burgraff
Photographer: Craig Anderson Photography
We also wish to thank Debbie Brown, Elizabeth Cecchettini, Susan Emerson, Joan Ford, Susan Lambur,
Nancy McClellan, Susan Meyer, Diane Tomlinson and Sue Voegtlin for their project creations and sewing.

Library of Congress Cataloging-in-Publication Data available on request.

This book printed on acid-free paper.
Printed in USA

10-9-8-7-6-5-4-3-2-1

ISBN 10: 1-890621-55-2
ISBN 13: 978-1-890621-55-1

Introduction

Travel will become a breeze after stitching up the fast and fabulous projects found on the following pages. Delight a favorite youngster with the cookies and crayons traveling totes or the comfy chenille rug—just two of the more than 12 quick projects you'll be inspired to try. Discover how easy quilt block patterns such as Four Patch and Pinwheel pair up with pre-printed panels to complete on-the-go accessories for a fun-filled kid's room.

Begin by purchasing a simple pre-printed panel design that's ideal for use "as is." (Quilt shops and fabric stores offer a wide variety of panel styles and colors.) Refer to the *Basics* section on pages 8–19 for ideas on how to embellish and finish it fast! Start by adding borders to a solo pre-printed fabric panel. Then go beyond basic to combine panels with patchwork, panel motifs with patchwork, and panel fabric coordinates with patchwork. You'll find projects that are quick and easy—quilts, pillows, wall décor—and even a toy trunk embellished with coordinating fabric.

Whether you're already comfortable working with fabric and have "made friends" with your sewing machine, or you're new to sewing and quilting, experience the joy that comes from using pre-printed panels to quickly create bright and artful projects every kid will love.

About the Artist

Inspired by her father, talented artist, Janet Wecker-Frisch has been drawing and painting since childhood. She translated her irresistible watercolor illustrations into her own line of ceramic ornaments. Their success led to licenses for wallpaper and border décor, and fabrics. Janet's *Hungry Animal Alphabet*© characters are the inspiration for a best-selling fabric collection created for South Sea Imports®. New collections *Good Ship Noah*©, *Camp Christmas*© and *Grounded In Love*© join Janet's other popular collections *Patches & Rhymes*© Mother Goose storybook characters, *Snowfolk Tea Party*©, *Circus Menagerie*© and *Noah's Ark*©.

Janet paints in a studio in her home which she shares with her husband, David. Located in House Springs, Missouri, a suburb of St. Louis, their home is often frequented by visits from their grown children—David, Jacqueline and Katie—and granddaughters Kaylan and Sydney.

Good Ship Noah©
Fabric Collection

Camp Christmas©
Fabric Collection

Circus Menagerie©
Fabric Collection

Patches & Rhymes©
Fabric Collection

Snowfolk
Tea Party©
Fabric
Collection

Hungry Animal©
Fabric Collection

5

Contents

PANELS & MORE

COORDINATES WITH PATCHWORK

Basics

◆◆◆◆◆

Learning how to mix pre-printed panels with patchwork will give you more options for many hours of quilting fun—whether you're new to quilting or simply need a refresher. Start by getting acquainted with the many styles of pre-printed panels and their fabric coordinates. Discover how easy it is to make simple patchwork blocks and combine them with pre-printed panel motifs and fabric coordinates. In no time at all, you'll have a beautiful top ready to quilt.

What is a Pre-printed Panel?

A pre-printed panel (also known as "cheater cloth") is a large piece of fabric with a stamped design often featuring a familiar theme such as the Good Ship Noah© and Camp Christmas© panels shown on these two pages. Frequently the center motif sets the scene for the "story" or theme which is carried out to the fabric edge and repeated in coordinating fabrics with prints, stripes, dots, checks, plaids and all-over "tosses." Accompanying borders ranging from simple to elaborate complete the collection. To make the best use of a panel, be sure to purchase any and all available coordinates for more design possibilities.

What is a Holiday-themed Pre-printed Panel?

Mixing pre-printed panels with patchwork for festive quilts or wallhangings is a real time-saver during the hectic holiday season. Santa themes, such as the Camp Christmas© shown above, are immensely popular because they can be stitched up quickly to use in your own holiday decorating or as gifts. Look for charming fabric coordinates that can be used for smaller seasonal accessories like table runners and place mats. The coordinating snowflakes, pine needles and buffalo check fabrics, as well as the rustic camp "accessory" fabric combine in projects that can be used throughout the winter season.

What is a Flannel Pre-printed Panel?

Recent improvements in heat-stamping designs onto fabric have made it possible to get excellent detail even on "fuzzy" fabrics such as flannel or fleece.

Since flannel's softness is most often associated with infants or toddlers, the pre-printed panel designs are themed accordingly. Traditional pink and baby blue are still in vogue, but bright pastels and even blue and red are quite popular. For baby shower or charity quilt gifts, soft green and yellow are a mainstay. Most often the pre-printed panel in flannel is the size of a standard receiving blanket, like the alphabet panel from the Hungry Animal© flannel collection, above.

What are Pre-printed Panel Possibilities?

New quiltmakers find panels ideal for practicing basic quiltmaking techniques. Experienced quiltmakers may already have discovered that pairing pre-printed panels with patchwork is perfect for kids' rooms collections, personalized birthday and holiday gifts or a fast-finish charity quilt.

When considering the purchase of a pre-printed panel fabric collection, look closely at the overall design. A successful pre-printed panel design should incorporate a wide array of characters or stand-alone "motifs" which can be cut out of the panel to mix with patchwork to give the appearance of appliqué.

What Is Patchwork?

Patchwork is any design made of odd pieces of cloth sewn together. Also known as piecing, small cuts of fabric are combined to form blocks that subsequently make up a quilt top.

The quilt top, batting and a backing are layered to form a "sandwich" that is held together by quilting or tying, and then finished with binding along the edges.

Historically, because used clothing was often the only available fabric from which to piece together a bed covering, a creative quiltmaker patched fabrics together to form particular patterns with more visual interest.

Today, an abundant variety of fabrics and techniques offers the quiltmaker endless opportunities for creative sewing expression.

Pre-printed panels are one of many products available today that make it easy to construct a quilt and other decorative accessories.

Many of the projects in this book utilize classic quilt block patterns such as those shown at right.

Pinwheel

Nine-Patch

Pinwheel – The similarity to the blades of a windmill or whirligig, gives the pinwheel block its name. The block is pieced from four half-square triangle patches positioned to appear as though they are spinning.

Nine-Patch – Another very traditional block, this simple design is just what its name implies—nine fabric patches. Rather than cutting nine individual fabric squares, construct this block following the easy-cut/easy-sew method: Use a rotary cutter to strip-cut three long fabric pieces; sew the strips together; and then cut the strips into units to sew the nine-patch block.

Mixing Pre-Printed Panels with Patchwork

To get you started, here are some ideas for creatively combining pre-printed panels and patchwork (pieced) blocks. Use your imagination to develop your own unique designs.

1. Make pieced blocks from small fabric panels. Border each block with complementary fabric strips to create sashing. Or add sashing with small fabric squares at each corner, creating cornerstones.

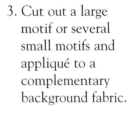

2. From a small panel cut out one motif from the design. Appliqué this shape to a background fabric or block.

3. Cut out a large motif or several small motifs and appliqué to a complementary background fabric.

4. Choose a motif to place in the center of a block. Called "fussy-cutting," this is how you can select a design to emphasize in your quilt block. Consider adding sashing to make the block larger.

Rotary Cutting

Rotary cutting is a quick-cutting method for making fabric pieces. Special rotary cutting tools have been designed to make cutting fabric easy and accurate.

For successful quick-cutting, always use a specially designed ruler, mat and rotary cutter. These items make cutting easier:

1. 6-1/2" x 6-1/2" rotary cutting ruler

2. 6-1/2" x 18" (or 6" x 18") rotary cutting ruler

3. Rotary cutter (45 mm or 60 mm)

4. Cutting mat (at least 24" in length or width)

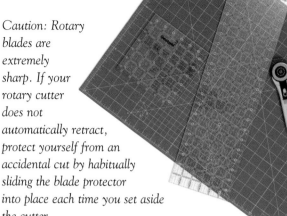

Caution: Rotary blades are extremely sharp. If your rotary cutter does not automatically retract, protect yourself from an accidental cut by habitually sliding the blade protector into place each time you set aside the cutter.

Straightening and Cutting Fabric

Hold the fabric upright to shake out the folds, adjust the edges, and align the selvages. Fold the fabric through the crosswise grain to make the selvages meet, and lay it on your cutting mat. Smooth the fabric, keeping the selvages aligned. Notice that the cut edges—the raw edges—of your fabric may not be aligned.

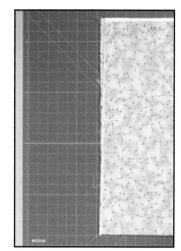

Straightening Fabric

To straighten the fabric edge, use a 6-1/2" square small ruler as a guide to place a 6-1/2" x 24"-long ruler straight on the crosswise fabric grain.

1. Lay the small ruler along the folded edge, placing one of the marked lines on the fold, and the left side of the small ruler near the fabric raw edge.

2. Place the long ruler beside, and to the left, of the small ruler, butting them together smoothly. The right edge of the long ruler should lay against the left edge of the small ruler.

Cutting Fabric

3. When the rulers are aligned with the fabric fold, pull away the small ruler, keeping your left hand on the long ruler to hold it in position. The long ruler should be positioned so its right edge is inside the raw edge of the fabric. Make sure both layers of the folded fabric will be cut when the small ruler is pulled away.

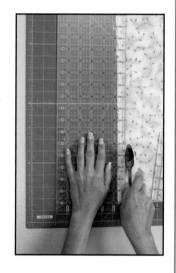

4. Hold the rotary cutter in a vertical position, and with steady pressure roll it along the right edge of the long ruler, from the bottom to the top. As the cutter rolls, walk your fingertips across the surface of the long ruler, maintaining pressure that holds the ruler in place while the rotary blade pushes against it.

When the rotary cutter reaches the top, the raw edge of the cross-grain has been cut and straightened.

After the fabric edge has been straightened, you're ready to begin cutting strips and pieces according to the project you've chosen to make.

Layering and Basting a Quilt

When you have finished your quilt top, it's time to make it into a quilt. A quilt sandwich is made by layering the completed quilt top, quilt batting and quilt backing. The layers are held together with safety pins, called pin basting, until the tying or quilting is completed.

Loft

The loft (thickness) and density of the batting are factors that determine whether you will tie or machine quilt the quilt's layers together. As a general rule, choose less than 1/2" loft polyester batting if you prefer a puffier look that's best for tying together with regularly-placed knots. Choose a low loft—no more than 1/4" thick—batting if you prefer a flatter appearance. Consider that low-loft cotton batting will move better beneath your sewing machine presser foot than a thicker loft batting. If you're uncertain about which batting to purchase, ask a shop clerk for a recommendation.

Layering the Quilt Sandwich

To layer the quilt sandwich you'll need:

1. A hard surface work area, preferably at least as large as the quilt backing.

Note: The tips of safety pins can scratch the work surface, so choose a hard surface that's scratch-resistant. Or, protect the work surface with a rotary mat.

2. A pressed quilt top with all seams laying flat.

3. Batting that measures 4" larger than the quilt top.

4. A pressed backing that measures 4" larger than the quilt top.

5. A roll of masking tape

6. Safety pins (1" to 1-1/2" in size).

Be sure the backing fabric has been well-pressed. Then, with the wrong side up, lay it on the surface. Smooth the fabric from the center outward.

To hold the backing securely to the surface, place masking tape on one edge toward the middle. On the opposite side, do the same, being sure not to pull the fabric too tightly.

Complete taping on these two sides. Repeat the process on the remaining two sides, taping every six inches.

Lay the batting on top of the quilt backing, carefully smoothing it from the center outward.

Lay the quilt top on the batting. Be sure that the quilt top and the batting are within the edges of the quilt backing. Check and re-check this before beginning to baste.

Pin-Basting the Quilt Sandwich

Safety pins are a quick way to baste a quilt and will hold a quilt sandwich together until the quilt is machine quilted or tied. Safety pins are best for basting when you expect to accomplish quilting in a short period of time.

Plan to baste with thread when you expect to hand quilt—a quilting process that takes more time to accomplish. For thread basting, use a sharp needle and thread, and large running stitches made in a spoke wheel or regular grid pattern. An advantage of thread basting is that thread may be left in a quilt for a longer period of time, whereas safety pins, when left in a quilt sandwich may leave permanent marks or stains.

Basting With Safety Pins

Open and scatter safety pins across the quilt top. With your dominant hand, insert a safety pin into the quilt top, through all layers of the quilt sandwich. Use both hands to close the safety pin. Pins can also be closed with a Kwik Clip™ or other tool such as a grapefruit spoon, held in your non-dominant hand. Insert safety pins randomly, every four to five inches apart across the quilt top to secure the backing.

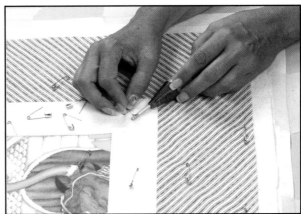

Quilting by Machine

Machine quilting is a quick and attractive way to quilt. If you've safety pin basted your quilt sandwich, be sure to remove the pins as you approach the area you want to quilt. Don't attempt to sew over the safety pins.

Two machine quilting options are available if you choose to quilt it yourself. You can either sew all straight-line stitches using a walking foot, or you can free-motion stitch, sewing curves, circles and other random shapes using only your hands to guide the fabric. For free-motion quilting you'll need a quilting foot.

Sewing Machine Set-up for Quilting

If you plan to straight-line machine quilt, attach a walking foot to your sewing machine. If you don't have a walking foot, use your machine's straight-stitch foot. For free-motion quilting, attach a darning foot. You'll also need to lower the feed dogs (refer to your sewing machine owner's manual), or cover them so you can move the quilt sandwich smoothly beneath the needle.

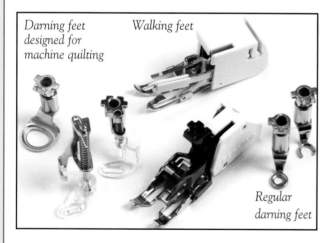

Darning feet designed for machine quilting

Walking feet

Regular darning feet

Needle for Machine Quilting

Change your sewing machine needle to a quilting needle or a jean's needle, size 80 or 90. This needle has a larger shaft that will more readily puncture the three layers of the quilt sandwich.

Thread for Machine Quilting

Choose nylon monofilament thread for machine quilting if you want to sew nearly invisible quilting stitches. Thread your sewing machine with the monofilament thread on top and for the bobbin choose a thread color that closely matches the quilt backing. Or, choose the same color of thread for the top and the bobbin. It's helpful to test your stitches before beginning to quilt. Make sure your sewing machine tension is adjusted for your thread (refer to your sewing machine owner's manual).

Design Options for Machine Quilting—Straight-Line or Free-Motion

Simple, straight-line machine quilting, also called utility quilting, is easy to accomplish and will hold the quilt layers together. Whenever possible, begin quilting from the center outward to prevent wrinkles from being quilted into the quilt top or back. Choose from one of these straight stitching options:

1. *Stitch-in-the-ditch quilting.* This quilting requires no marking. Simply stitch along the seam lines as closely as possible.

 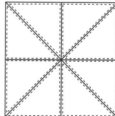

2. *Grid quilting.* Sew a simple grid at regularly spaced intervals on the quilt surface. Align a long rotary ruler with the intersections of blocks. Lightly draw quilting lines with chalk, marking pencil or a washout pen. Quilt on the lines.

 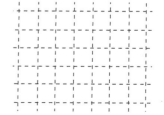

Free-motion quilting is a bit more challenging, but definitely fun. Lower the feed dogs and use a quilting foot for:

3. *Echo quilting.* After you've stitched to outline a motif, move outward and repeat the quilted outline at regular intervals.

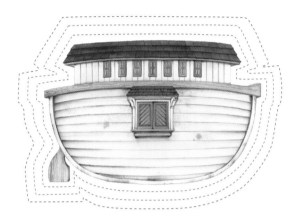

4. *Stipple quilting.* (This is also known as meander quilting.) No marking is needed to create these random curves that flow across a quilt surface.

For greater visual interest, try a combination of several quilting designs including straight-line, stitch-in-the-ditch and free-motion quilting.

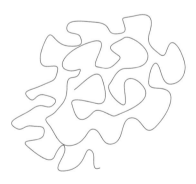

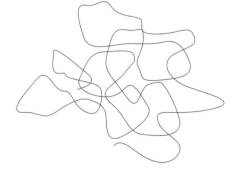

Binding a Quilt

The last step in finishing your quilt is to add the binding. Binding is a fabric strip that encases the outside edges of the quilt. Double-fold binding is most commonly made because it's durable. As the name implies, the quilt edge is wrapped with two layers of fabric. A 2-1/4" to 2-1/2"-wide fabric strip, is folded and sewn to the front of the quilt along the edge, then folded and hand sewn to the quilt back.

If your quilt will hang on the wall, add a sleeve to the top edge of the quilt back at the same time the binding is sewn.

Piecing Binding

If you've cut the binding strips according to the pattern instructions, you'll need to sew strips together to obtain the length needed. Here's how:

1. Position a binding strip, right side up, horizontally in front of you.

2. To the left and at a perpendicular angle to the horizontal strip, position another binding strip right side down on top of the horizontal strip.

3. From corner to corner, across the overlapping areas, draw a diagonal line.

4. Sew on the drawn line.

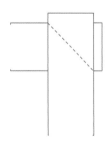

5. Trim away the excess fabric to measure a 1/4" seam allowance.

6. Press open the sewn seam to reduce bulk.

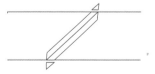

7. Fold wrong sides together and press.

Sewing the Binding to the Quilt Top

Align the raw edges of the binding strip to the raw edge of the quilt top. Sew the binding to the quilt top, using a 1/4" seam allowance.

Trimming the Quilt Sandwich

After machine sewing the binding to the quilt sandwich, cut away excess fabric and batting. Exercise caution! Be sure to cut away only the excess—not the folded binding or the binding corners.

Place the quilt on the cutting mat with the binding on top. Use the long rotary ruler to measure 3/8" outward from the binding stitching line. Rotary cut along the ruler to remove all but 3/8" of the backing and batting.

Overview of Continuous Binding with Mitered Corners

This binding is applied in one long, continuous fabric strip. By folding the binding at each corner, extra fabric is allowed to hand sew a miter into the corner.

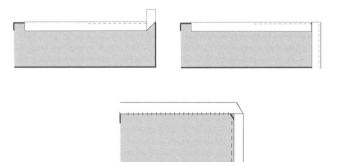

Hand Sewing the Binding to the Quilt Back

After trimming away any excess material on the quilt edge, hand sew the binding in place. Lay the quilt on your lap with the backing facing up. Fold and secure the binding to the back of the quilt using metal hair clips.

Knot one end of a needle with thread that matches the color of the quilt backing. Begin hand sewing at any point, securing the binding fold over the machine stitches. Stitch from right to left using a slip stitch.

Take care at each corner to fold and tuck fabric into a diagonal seam, hand sewing it into place. When the binding and four corners have been sewn down on the quilt back, turn the quilt over and hand sew the front side of each mitered-corner seam.

If you've added a sleeve to your quilt, also hand sew the folded edge of the sleeve to the quilt back, making sure to take stitches that will not show on the quilt front.

Adding a Hanging Sleeve to a Quilt

To display a quilt on a wall, the best time to add a sleeve or rod pocket to the quilt is at the same time that binding is sewn to the quilt.

The instructions that follow are for creating a sleeve that holds a hidden rod. When the quilt is hung on the wall, nothing is visible except the quilt.

Depending on the size of the quilt you're hanging, you'll need to determine what width of flat lath or molding, or the diameter of the dowel rod you'll need that will reliably support the quilt's weight. A 1" to 2"-wide board gives good support and keeps a quilt flat against the wall. For small quilts, try using a wooden yardstick as a sleeve rod.

Measure, Cut and Add a Sleeve

1. Decide which way you want to hang the quilt and measure across the top.

2. Deduct 2" from this number to obtain the finished length of the sleeve.

3. Add 3" to the finished length to obtain the unfinished length. This measurement allows a 1-1/2" fold at each sleeve end.

4. Measure the width of the lath, molding or dowel used to hang the quilt. Multiply the width by 2, add 1" for ease of insertion and 1/2" for seam allowances to determine the unfinished width of the sleeve.

5. Using the unfinished measurements, cut out a sleeve from the same fabric as the quilt backing.

6. At each end of the sleeve make a 1-1/2" fold to the wrong side; press.

7. Fold the sleeve length in half, wrong sides together; press.

8. Align the raw edges of the sleeve with the top raw edge of the quilt back. Be sure the sleeve is positioned on the back of the quilt; pin.

9. Align the raw edges of the binding to the top raw edges of the quilt front; pin.

10. Attach the binding and sleeve to the quilt top with a 1/4" seam allowance.

11. Using a slip stitch, hand sew the folded edge of the sleeve to the quilt back. Avoid taking stitches that will show on the quilt front. Finish by sewing the binding to the back of the quilt.

Measure, Cut, Drill and Hang a Board

1. Deduct 1" from the measurement of the quilt top and cut a 1" to 2-1/2"-wide, flat board that length.

2. Approximately 1/3" to 1/2" from each end of the board, drill a hole that will accommodate a nail head.

3. Position the board on the wall and mark the location of the drilled holes.

4. Hammer nails through the marks.

5. Insert the drilled board through the sleeve.

6. Hang the quilt.

Measure, Cut and Hang a Dowel Rod

1. Deduct 1" from the measurement of the quilt top and cut a dowel that length.

2. Position the dowel to place marks on the wall 1/4" to 1/3" in from each end of the dowel.

3. Hammer nails through these marks.

4. Insert the dowel rod through the sleeve.

5. Hang the dowel on the nails, making sure the quilt edges cover the nail heads.

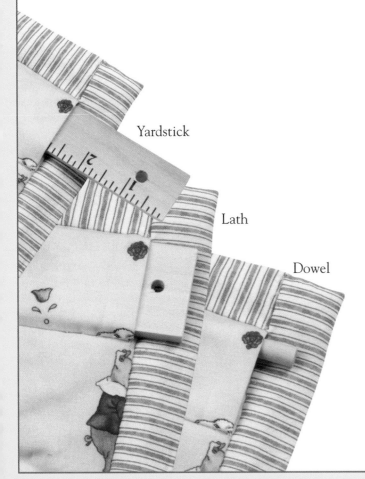

Yardstick

Lath

Dowel

Prairie Points Quilt

Prairie points, pinwheels and animal stripe blocks surround a pre-printed panel, turning it into a fun and colorful child's quilt.

◆◆◆◆◆

Materials

Finished size: 55x67"

27-1/2x42-1/2" rectangle
from pre-printed character quilt panel

1-1/4 yards of animal stripe fabric
for pieced border

3/4 yard of blue plaid fabric
for prairie points, C, F and I strips
and pinwheel blocks

3/4 yard of green plaid fabric
for prairie points, A, H and J strips
and pinwheel blocks

5/8 yard of red plaid fabric
for prairie points, B and E strips
and pinwheel blocks

1/2 yard of yellow plaid fabric
for prairie points, D and G strips
and pinwheel blocks

3-1/4 yards of all-over check fabric
for backing

56x68" piece of quilt batting

Cut the Fabric

From the animal stripe, cut:
> 10—4-1/2x44" strips;
> from the strips cut 84—4-1/2" border squares

From blue plaid, cut:
> 2—3-1/2x44" strips;
> from the strips cut 23—3-1/2" prairie point squares
> 4—2x44" strips; from the strips cut 1—2x30-1/2" C strip
> and reserve the remaining
> 4—4-7/8" block squares

From green plaid, cut:
> 2—3-1/2x44" strips;
> from the strips cut 23—3-1/2" prairie point squares
> 4—2x44" strips; from the strips cut 1—2x42-1/2" A strip,
> 1—2x33-1/2" H strip and reserve the remaining
> 4—4-7/8" block squares

From red plaid, cut:
> 2—3-1/2x44" strips;
> from the strips cut 23—3-1/2" prairie point squares
> 3—2x44" strips; from the strips cut 1—2x42-1/2" B strip
> and reserve the remaining
> 4—4-7/8" block squares

From yellow plaid, cut:
> 2—3-1/2x44" strips;
> from the strips cut 23—3-1/2" prairie point squares
> 2—2x44" strips;
> from the strips cut 1—2x30-1/2" D strip and 1—2x33-1/2" G strip
> 4—4-7/8" block squares

From all-over check fabric, cut:

    2—34-1/2x56" backing rectangles

Sew with right sides together using 1/4" seam allowances unless otherwise specified.

Instructions

Assemble the Quilt Center

1. Sew the short ends of the remaining 2"-wide blue plaid strips together to form one long strip. Press the seam allowances open. Repeat with the remaining 2"-wide green plaid strips and the remaining 2"-wide red plaid strips. From the pieced strips, cut 1—2x45-1/2" blue plaid F strip 1—2x48-1/2" blue plaid I strip, 1—2x48-1/2" green plaid J strip and 1—2x45-1/2" red plaid E strip.

2. Use the Quilt Assembly Diagram on page 23 as a guide to assemble the quilt center. Sew the green plaid A strip to the left edge of the 27-1/2x42-1/2" pre-printed character quilt panel and the red plaid B strip to the right edge. Press the seam allowances away from the center.

3. Sew the blue plaid C strip to the top edge of the quilt panel and the yellow plaid D strip to the bottom edge. Press the seam allowances away from the center.

4. Sew the red plaid E strip to the left edge of the quilt and the blue plaid F strip to the right edge. Press the seam allowances away from the center.

5. Sew the yellow plaid G strip to the top edge of the quilt and the green plaid H strip to the bottom edge. Press the seam allowances away from the center.

6. Sew the blue plaid I strip to the left edge of the quilt and the green plaid J strip to the right edge. Press the seam allowances away from the center.

Assemble the Pinwheel Blocks

1. With right sides together layer the 4-7/8" plaid squares in pairs, using a blue plaid with each of the yellow plaids and a green plaid with each of the red plaids. Cut the layered squares in half diagonally as shown in Diagram A to make 16 sets of triangles.

Diagram A

2. Sew 1/4" from the diagonal edge of each pair as shown in Diagram B to make a square. Press open with the seam allowances toward the darker fabric.

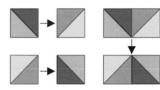

Diagram B

3. Arrange sets of four squares as shown in Diagram C. Sew the squares together in rows and then sew the rows together to make 4 pinwheel blocks.

Diagram C

Assemble the Quilt Top

1. Sew together four rows of 9—4-1/2" animal stripe squares for the top and bottom pieced borders, alternating the direction of the stripes from square to square. Begin and end two of the rows with the stripes running vertically; press the seam allowances to the left. Begin and end two of the rows with the stripes running horizontally; press the seam allowances to the right.

2. Sew the rows together in pairs as shown in Diagram D for the top and bottom pieced borders. Press the seam allowances in one direction.

Diagram D

3. Sew together four rows of 12—4-1/2" animal stripe squares for the side-pieced borders, in the same manner as for the top and bottom pieced borders in Step 1.

4. Sew the rows together in pairs for the side-pieced borders. Press the seam allowances in one direction.

5. Sew the side-pieced borders to the left and right edges of the quilt. Press the seam allowances toward the center.

6. Sew a pinwheel block to each end of the top and bottom pieced borders. Press the seam allowances toward the borders. Sew the borders to the top and bottom edges of the quilt. Press the seam allowances toward the center.

Complete the Quilt

1. For the prairie points, refer to Diagram E. Fold each 3-1/2" plaid square in half diagonally with wrong sides facing and press. Fold in half again, forming a smaller triangle and press.

Diagram E

2. Pin the prairie points to the right side of the quilt top in the desired color order, aligning the long raw edge of each prairie point with the raw edge of the quilt top. Begin at the corner of an edge, overlapping the points slightly as shown in Diagram F by slipping the folded edge of a prairie point into the open side of the adjacent triangle. Adjust the overlap as needed to fit 25 points on each side edge and 20 on the top and bottom edges; there are two extra prairie points. Sew the points to the quilt top.

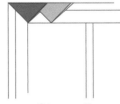

Diagram F

3. Sew together the long edges of the 34-1/2x56" backing rectangles with a 1/2" seam allowance. Press the seam allowances to one side.

4. Smooth out the backing on a flat surface with the wrong side up and center the batting on the backing. Center the quilt top, right side up, on top of the batting. Baste the layers together.

5. Beginning in the center and working outward, machine quilt through all layers as desired. Our quilt was machine quilted along the design lines of the pre-printed quilt panel and in the ditch along the outer edges of the strips and the pinwheel blocks. In addition, a feather design is centered on each pinwheel block and the remaining areas are filled with freehand quilting.

6. Trim the backing and batting even with the raw edge of the quilt top. Trim an additional 1/4" of batting from each edge. Turn the prairie points out to point away from the quilt top, folding the raw edges of the quilt top over onto the batting. Fold under 1/4" on the edges of the backing. Slip stitch the folded edge of the backing in place or sew in the ditch along the prairie points, catching the folded edge of backing on the back of the quilt.

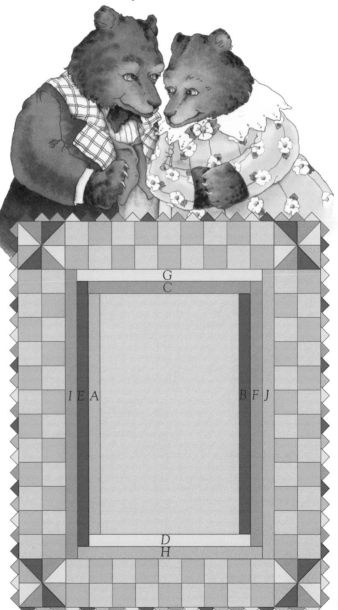

Quilt Assembly Diagram

Storybook Quilt

Wrap up in a good book. It's easy when your favorite quilt tells the tale. A pre-printed book panel and four-patch blocks team up to make a storybook quilt.

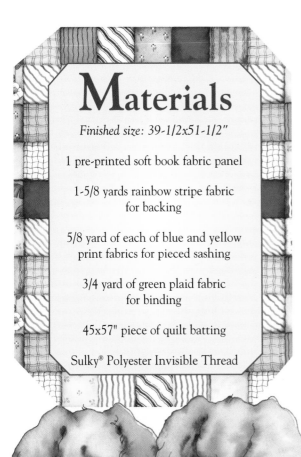

Materials

Finished size: 39-1/2x51-1/2"

1 pre-printed soft book fabric panel

1-5/8 yards rainbow stripe fabric for backing

5/8 yard of each of blue and yellow print fabrics for pieced sashing

3/4 yard of green plaid fabric for binding

45x57" piece of quilt batting

Sulky® Polyester Invisible Thread

Cut the Fabric

From soft book fabric panel, cut:
    12—9-1/2" block squares

From rainbow stripe fabric, cut:
    1—44x57" backing rectangle

From blue print, cut:
    10—2x44" strips; from the strips cut 31—2x9-1/2" sashing strips and 40—2" sashing squares

From yellow print, cut:
    10—2x44" strips; from the strips cut 31—2x9-1/2" sashing strips and 40—2" sashing squares

From green plaid, cut:
    2-1/4"-wide bias strips to total 195" of binding

Sew with right sides together using 1/4" seam allowances unless otherwise specified.

Instructions

Assemble the Sashing

1. Using one of each color, sew the long edges of the 2x9-1/2" blue and yellow print strips together in pairs for the pieced sashing. Press the seam allowances toward the blue strips.

2. Arrange sets of four 2" squares as shown in Diagram A, using two blue and two yellow for each set. Sew the squares together in rows and then sew the rows together to make 20 pieced sashing squares.

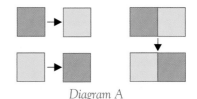

Diagram A

25

Assemble the Quilt Top

1. Lay out the block squares, and pieced sashing and sashing squares on a flat surface, using the Quilt Assembly Diagram as a guide.

2. To make the block rows, sew together the block squares and pieced sashing as indicated in Diagram B. Press all seam allowances in one direction.

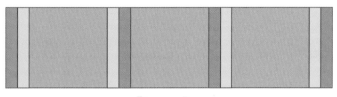

Diagram B

3. To make the sashing rows, sew together the sashing strips and sashing squares as indicated in Diagram C. Press all seam allowances the opposite direction from the block rows.

Diagram C

4. Sew the block rows and sashing rows together; press.

Complete the Quilt

1. Smooth out the backing on a flat surface with the wrong side up and center the batting on the backing. Center the quilt top, right side up, on top of the batting. Baste the layers together.

2. Thread your machine with invisible thread and machine quilt through all layers beginning in the center and working outward. Our quilt was machine quilted along the design lines of the pre-printed block squares and in the ditch along the edges of the block squares. In addition, the blue print sashing pieces were filled with meander quilting.

3. Sew the short ends of the 2-1/4"-wide binding strips together with diagonal seams to form one long binding strip. Trim the excess fabric, leaving 1/4" seam allowances. Press the seam allowances open. Fold the strip in half lengthwise with wrong sides together; press.

4. Beginning at the center of one edge of the quilt, place the binding strip on the right side of the quilt top, aligning the raw edges of the binding with the raw edges of the quilt top. Fold over the beginning of the binding strip about 1/2". Sew through all layers 1/4" from the raw edges, mitering the corners. Trim away the excess binding, leaving 1/2" at the end to overlap the beginning of the strip. Trim the batting and backing even with the quilt top.

5. Fold the binding to the back of the quilt to cover the machine stitching; press. Slip stitch the folded edge of the binding in place or sew in the ditch along the binding, catching the folded edge of binding on the back of the quilt.

Quilt Assembly Diagram

Storytime Book

*Share this panel book with a child
and a happy ending is sure to follow.*

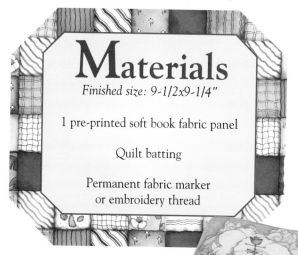

Materials

Finished size: 9-1/2x9-1/4"

1 pre-printed soft book fabric panel

Quilt batting

Permanent fabric marker
or embroidery thread

Cut the Fabric

From the pre-printed panel, cut:
  6 double-pages as indicated
  by the dashed lines

From quilt batting, cut:
  3—10x20" rectangles

Instructions

1. Personalize the back cover if desired with a fabric marker
   or embroidery.

2. Smooth out a batting rectangle on a flat surface. Center
   pages 12/1, right side up, on the batting. Center pages
   2/11, right side down, on pages 12/1. Sew the pages and
   batting together on the solid line approximately 1/4"
   from the raw edge; leave a 4" opening on the bottom
   edge for turning. Trim the corners and turn right side out.
   Press, turning under the seam allowances of the opening.
   Sew the opening closed to complete Page Set 1.

3. Repeat Step 2 for the remaining pages, pairing pages
   10/3 with 4/9 for page Set 2 and pages 8/5 with 6/7 for
   Page Set 3.

4. Place Page Set 1 on a flat surface with Noah/Zebra
   facing up. Place Page Set 2 on Page Set 1 with the
   Camel/Rhinoceros facing up. Place Page Set 3 on
   Page Set 2 with the Giraffe/Hippopotamus facing up.
   Check to be sure the animals are in alphabetical order.
   Sew through all layers at the center.

Travel Totes

*Ready, set, go! These easy-to-make-and-carry
totes will make any road trip a breeze. Filled
with crayons, crackers or other toddler favorites
these totes go the distance.*

Papier-mâché box with lid

Fabric for box lid and base

Pre-printed fussy-cut fabric

Pencil

Tape measure

Spray adhesive

Instructions

Place the box lid, top side down, on the wrong side
of the fabric. Use a pencil to draw around the lid. Cut
out the lid shape 1/2" beyond the drawn line. Apply
spray adhesive to the wrong side of the fabric shape.
Center the fabric shape, adhesive side down, on the lid
and smooth from the center out. Fold the excess fabric
onto the lid sides, using scissors to clip as needed.

Find the circumference of the lid with a tape
measure; add 1" for overlap. Measure the height of the
lid; add 1/2". Use these measurements to cut a fabric
strip for the sides of the lid. Apply spray adhesive onto
wrong side of fabric strip. Press the strip onto the lid
sides so it extends 1/2" beyond the lid bottom. Wrap
the excess fabric around the bottom edge of the lid and
adhere to the inside.

Find the circumference of the box base; add 1" for
overlap. Measure the height of the base; add 1/2". Use
these measurements to cut fabric for the base sides.
Apply spray adhesive to the wrong side of the fabric
piece. Press the fabric onto the base sides, keeping the
bottom edge of the fabric even with the base bottom.
Fold the excess fabric around the top edge of the lid
and adhere to the inside.

To embellish box, fussy-cut motifs from pre-printed
fabric. Spray adhesive onto the wrong side of the motifs
and press onto lid and base in desired locations.

Pinwheel Quilt

Finish a classic Pinwheel block quilt with style by fussy-cutting elements of a pre-printed fabric panel and appliquéing them to the quilt top.

Materials

Finished size: 43x56"

1 pre-printed character quilt panel for appliqués

2/3 yard of assorted pre-printed coordinating fabrics fussy-cut for appliqués

1-1/2 yards of red plaid fabric for blocks, sashing squares and binding

1-1/4 yards of all-over check fabric for sashing

1/4 yard each of plaid fabric in blue, green and yellow for blocks

1/4 yard each of small print fabric in blue, green and yellow for blocks

1-3/4 yards of blue large print for backing

Paper-backed fusible webbing

Sulky® Tear-Easy™ stabilizer

Sulky® KK 2000 temporary spray adhesive

Sulky® Rayon or Poly Deco™ Decorative Thread in blue, green, red, white and yellow

44x58" piece of quilt batting

Sulky® Polyester Invisible Thread

Cut the Fabric

From the pre-printed quilt panel and assorted coordinating fabrics, fussy-cut:
    1 large ark and 13 smaller appliqué shapes, leaving about 1/2" around each shape

From red plaid, cut:
    2—5-7/8x44" strips;
    from the strips cut 12—5-7/8" block squares
    2—3-1/2x44" strips;
    from the strips cut 20—3-1/2" sashing squares
    2-1/2"-wide bias strips to total 220" of binding

From all-over check fabric, cut:
    11—3-1/2x44" strips;
    from the strips cut 31—3-1/2x10-1/2" sashing strips

From each blue, green and yellow plaid and small print, cut:
    1—5-7/8x44" strip;
    from the strip cut 6—5-7/8" block squares
    for a total of 36 block squares

From blue large print, cut:
    1—44x58" backing rectangle

Sew with right sides together using 1/4" seam allowances unless otherwise specified.

Instructions

Assemble the Pinwheel Blocks

1. With right sides together, layer the 5-7/8" squares in pairs, using a red plaid with each of the blue plaid and blue print squares, a yellow plaid with each of the green print squares, and a green plaid with each of the yellow print squares. Cut the layered squares in half diagonally as shown in Diagram A to make 48 sets of triangles.

Diagram A

2. Sew 1/4" from the diagonal edge of each pair as shown in Diagram B to make a square. Press the seam allowances toward the darker fabric.

Diagram B

3. Arrange sets of four squares as shown in Diagram C. Sew the squares together in rows and then sew the rows together to make 12 pinwheel blocks.

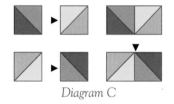

Diagram C

Assemble the Quilt Top

1. Lay out the pinwheel blocks, sashing strips and sashing squares on a flat surface, using the photograph and Quilt Assembly Diagram on page 31 as guides.

2. To make the block rows, sew together the pinwheel blocks and sashing strips as indicated in Diagram D. Press all seam allowances in one direction.

Diagram D

3. To make the sashing rows, sew together the sashing strips and sashing squares as indicated in Diagram E. Press all seam allowances the opposite direction from the block rows.

Diagram E

4. Sew the block rows and sashing rows together; press.

5. For each appliqué, cut a corresponding shape of fusible webbing. Fuse webbing to the wrong side of each appliqué shape, following the manufacturer's instructions. Carefully cut out the shapes and remove the paper backing.

6. Spread the quilt top right side up on a flat surface. Referring to the Quilt Assembly Diagram on page 31, position the appliqué shapes on the quilt. When you are pleased with the arrangement, fuse the shapes to the quilt.

7. Cut squares of tear-away stabilizer slightly larger than the fused shapes. Center a piece of stabilizer behind each fused shape on the back of the quilt top with temporary spray adhesive. Satin stitch over the edges of each shape with white decorative thread. For an added touch, use a second color of decorative thread to machine buttonhole stitch directly over the white satin stitching. Tear away the stabilizer.

Complete the Quilt

1. Smooth out the backing rectangle on a flat surface with the wrong side up and center the batting on the backing. Center the quilt top, right side up, on top of the batting. Baste the layers together.

2. Thread your machine with invisible thread and machine quilt through all layers beginning in the center and working outward. Quilt in the ditch along the outer edges of each appliqué. Quilt 3/8" from the edges of the triangles and sashing squares. In addition, quilt two lines to divide each sashing strip into thirds.

3. Sew the short ends of the 2-1/2"-wide binding strips together with diagonal seams to form one long

binding strip. Trim the excess fabric, leaving 1/4"
seam allowances. Press the seam allowances open.
Fold the strip in half lengthwise with wrong sides
together; press. Refer to Piecing Binding on page 17
for more detailed instructions.

4. Beginning at the center of one edge of the quilt,
    place the binding strip on the right side of the quilt
    top, aligning the raw edges of the binding with the
    raw edges of the quilt top. Fold over the beginning of
    the binding strip about 1/2". Sew through all
    layers 1/2" from the raw edges, mitering the corners.
    Trim away the excess binding, leaving 1/2" at the end
    to overlap the beginning of the strip. Trim
    the batting and backing even with the quilt top.

5. Fold the binding to the back of the quilt to cover
    the machine stitching; press. Slip-stitch the folded
    edge of the binding in place or sew in the ditch along
    the binding, catching the folded edge of
    binding on the back of the quilt.

Quilt Assembly Diagram

Two-by-Two Quilt

Zebras, lions, hippos, tigers and giraffes march across this bright quilt the same way they boarded the ark—two-by-two.

◆▪◆▪◆

Materials

Finished size: 40x48"

1 pre-printed character quilt panel

1-3/4 yards of all-over check fabric for backing and blocks

1 yard of red plaid fabric for inner border, blocks and binding

3/4 yard of blue print fabric for blocks

5/8 yard of rainbow stripe fabric for outer border

3/8 yard of blue plaid fabric for blocks

1/4 yard each of green and yellow plaid fabric for blocks

45x53" piece of quilt batting

Sulky® Polyester Invisible Thread

Cut the Fabric

From pre-printed panel, cut:
  10—6" animal character motifs

From all-over check, cut:
  1—44x53" backing rectangle
  2—4-1/2x44" strips; from the strips cut 10—4-1/2" A squares

From red plaid, cut:
  1—2-1/2x44" strip; from the strip cut 16—2-1/2" D squares
  4—1-1/2x44" strips; from the strips cut 2—1-1/2x36" top and bottom inner borders and 2—1-1/2x44" side inner borders
  2-1/4"-wide bias strips to total 190" of binding

From blue print, cut:
  5—4-1/2x44" strips; from the strips cut 40—4-1/2" squares; cut the squares diagonally in both directions to make 160 C triangles

From rainbow stripe, cut:
  5—3-1/2x44" outer border strips

From blue plaid, cut:
  4—5-1/4" squares; cut the squares diagonally in both directions to make 16 B triangles
  2—2-1/2x44" strips; from the strips cut 24—2-1/2" D squares

From green plaid, cut:
  6—5-1/4" squares; cut the squares diagonally in both directions to make 24 B triangles
  1—2-1/2x44" strip; from the strip cut 16—2-1/2" D squares

From yellow plaid, cut:
  2—2-1/2x44" strips; from the strips cut 24—2-1/2" D squares

Sew with right sides together using 1/4" seam allowances unless otherwise specified.

Instructions

Assemble the Square-in-Square Blocks

1. Sew four green plaid B triangles to each side of an A square as shown in Diagram A. Press the seam allowances toward the triangles.

Diagram A

2. Sew two blue print C triangles to two sides of a blue plaid D square as shown in Diagram B. Repeat to make a total of 4 C/D/C units.

Diagram B

3. Sew a C/D/C unit to each side of the A/B unit to complete a green/blue block as shown in Diagram C. Press all the seam allowances away from the center of the block. Make 6 green/blue blocks.

Diagram C

4. Repeat Steps 1-3, using blue plaid B triangles and green plaid D squares to make 4 blue/green blocks as shown in Diagram D.

Diagram D

Assemble the Character Blocks

1. Sew two blue print C triangles to two sides of a yellow plaid D square as shown in Diagram E. Repeat to make a total of 4 C/D/C units.

Diagram E

2. Sew a C/D/C unit to each side of a 6" animal character motif as shown in Diagram F. Press seam allowances away from the center of the block. Make 6 blue/yellow character blocks.

Diagram F

3. Repeat Steps 1–2, using red plaid D squares to make 4 blue/red character blocks as shown in Diagram G.

Diagram G

Assemble the Quilt Top

1. Lay out the square-in-square and character blocks in five rows of four blocks, using the photograph on page 32 and Quilt Assembly Diagram on page 35 as guides.

2. When you are pleased with the arrangement, sew the blocks together in rows to complete the quilt center. Press the seam allowances of each row to one side, alternating the direction with each row.

3. Sew the rows together to complete the quilt center; press.

4. To miter the inner border, center and pin a 1-1/2x36" red plaid inner border strip to the top and bottom edges of the quilt center. Sew together, beginning and ending the seam 1/4" from the side edges of the quilt center as shown in Diagram H. Press the seam allowances toward the border.

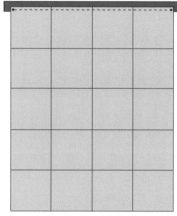

Diagram H

5. Sew the 1-1/2x44" red plaid inner border strips to the left and right edges of the quilt center as in Step 4.

6. Working with one corner at a time, draw a diagonal line on the wrong side of the top strip from the corner of the stitching to the point where the two strips meet at the raw edges as shown in Diagram I. Reposition strips so the bottom border is on top and draw a second line in the same manner.

Diagram I

7. With right sides together, match the drawn lines and pin as shown in Diagram J. Beginning at the inside corner, sew the inner border strips together directly on the drawn lines. Trim the excess fabric, leaving a 1/4" seam allowance. Press the seam allowances in one direction. Repeat Steps 4 and 5 to miter each corner.

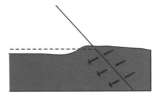

Diagram J

8. Sew the 3-1/2"-wide rainbow stripe outer border strips as needed to make two 44" lengths and two 52" lengths. Follow Steps 4 to 7 to attach the outer border and miter the corners, sewing the 44" lengths to the top and bottom edges and the 52" lengths to the left and right edges.

Complete the Quilt

1. Smooth out the backing rectangle on a flat surface with the wrong side up and center the batting on the backing. Center the quilt top, right side up, on top of the batting. Baste the layers together.

2. Thread your machine with invisible thread and machine quilt through all layers beginning in the center and working outward. Quilt in the ditch along all seams of the blocks and along both edges of the inner border. In addition, randomly quilt straight lines across the width of the outer border.

3. Sew the short ends of the 2-1/4"-wide binding strips together with diagonal seams to form one long binding strip. Trim the excess fabric, leaving 1/4" seam allowances. Press the seam allowances open. Fold the strip in half lengthwise with wrong sides together; press.

4. Beginning at the center of one edge of the quilt, place the binding strip on the right side of the quilt top, aligning the raw edges of the binding with the raw edges of the quilt top. Fold over the beginning of the binding strip about 1/2". Sew through all layers

1/4" from the raw edges, mitering the corners. Trim away the excess binding, leaving 1/2" at the end to overlap the beginning of the strip. Trim the batting and backing even with the quilt top.

5. Fold the binding to the back of the quilt to cover the machine stitching; press. Slip stitch the folded edge of the binding in place or sew in the ditch along the binding, catching the folded edge of binding on the back of the quilt.

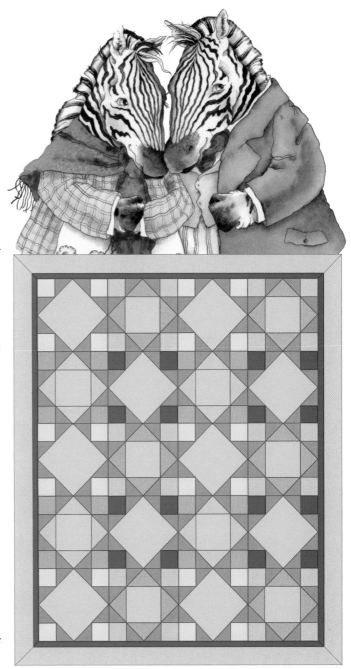

Quilt Assembly Diagram

Chenille Rug

This colorful chenille rug adds a feeling of fun to any youngster's room. Created by combining four simple, pre-printed panels, it's the perfect touch for the floor, rocker or even a wall.

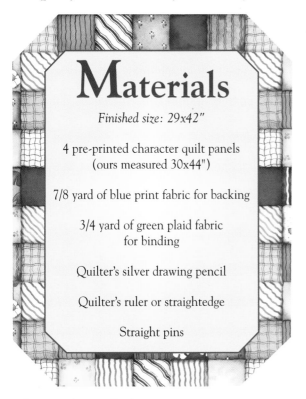

Materials

Finished size: 29x42"

4 pre-printed character quilt panels
(ours measured 30x44")

7/8 yard of blue print fabric for backing

3/4 yard of green plaid fabric
for binding

Quilter's silver drawing pencil

Quilter's ruler or straightedge

Straight pins

Cut the Fabric

For the quilt panels, trim 1/4" beyond the outer border.

From the blue print, use a trimmed quilt panel as a pattern
to cut one backing rectangle.

From the green plaid, cut:
2-1/2"-wide bias strips to total 150" of binding

Instructions

1. Smooth out one panel for the top layer on a flat surface, right side up. Use the drawing pencil and a quilter's ruler or straightedge to draw diagonal lines across the fabric, spacing lines 5/8" apart. Lines must be at a 45-degree angle from the fabric grain.

2. Smooth out the backing rectangle on a flat surface, wrong side up. Center the four quilt panels atop the backing rectangle, right sides up, with the marked panel on the top. To prevent any movement of the layered fabrics, use straight pins to pin all five layers together along the drawn lines. Sew on the drawn lines.

3. Carefully cut through the top three layers of fabric, cutting evenly between the stitching lines. Take care not to cut the bottom panel or the backing rectangle.

4. Sew the short ends of the 2-1/2"-wide green plaid binding strips together with diagonal seams to form one long binding strip. Trim the seam allowances to 1/4" and press open. Fold the strip in half lengthwise with wrong sides together; press.

5. Beginning at the center of one edge of the rug, place the binding strip on the right side, aligning the raw edges of the binding with the raw edges of the rug. Fold over the beginning of the binding strip about 1/2". Sew through all layers 1/4" from the raw edges, mitering the corners. Trim away the excess binding, leaving 1/2" at the end to overlap the beginning of the strip.

6. Fold the binding to the back of the rug to cover the machine stitching; press. Slip-stitch the folded edge of the binding in place or sew in the ditch along the binding, catching the folded edge of the binding on the back of the rug.

Rickrack Wallhanging

A convenient, pre-printed fabric panel embellished with bright rickrack and coordinating buttons makes a quick-to-sew wallhanging.

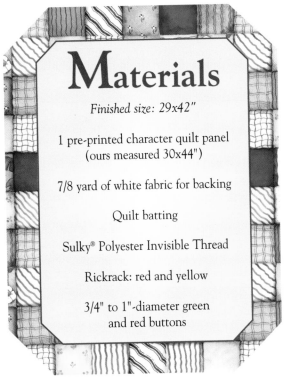

Materials

Finished size: 29x42"

1 pre-printed character quilt panel
(ours measured 30x44")

7/8 yard of white fabric for backing

Quilt batting

Sulky® Polyester Invisible Thread

Rickrack: red and yellow

3/4" to 1"-diameter green
and red buttons

Cut the Fabric

For the quilt panel, trim the left, right and top edges 1/4" beyond the outer border and the bottom edge 1/2" beyond the character diamond-shaped blocks.

From white, cut:
　　1—32x44" backing rectangle

From batting, cut:
　　1—32x44" rectangle

Instructions

1. Smooth out the batting rectangle on a flat surface and center the white backing, right side up, on top of the batting. Center the trimmed quilt panel, right side down, on the backing. Pin the layers together.

2. Sew the layers together 1/4" from the trimmed edges of the panel, leaving a 10" opening in the top edge. Trim the batting and backing even with the quilt panel. Clip the corners and turn the wall quilt right side out. Sew the opening closed.

3. Thread your sewing machine with invisible thread and quilt as desired. Our wall quilt was machine quilted to outline the ark, the banner, the character blocks and the small diamonds between the character blocks.

4. Sew yellow rickrack along the side and top edges of the quilt front, centering the rickrack over the inside edge of the outer border. Sew red rickrack along the bottom edge of the quilt front. Sew buttons on the rickrack, referring to the photo below for placement suggestions.

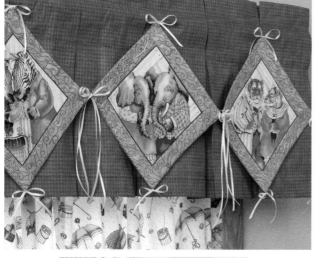

Diamond Delights

Dress up a valance with these delightful bordered-character cut-outs.

Materials

Finished size: 8-1/2x8-1/2"

1 pre-printed character quilt panel

Blue print fabric for border and backing

Fusible fleece

1/8"-wide white satin ribbon

Sulky® Polyester Invisible Thread

Cut the Fabric

From pre-printed panel, cut:
> 6-3/4" diamond-shaped character squares

From blue print, cut:
> 4—1-3/4x8" border strips for each character square
> 1—9-1/4" backing square for each character square

From fusible fleece, cut:
> 1—9-1/4" square for each character square

Sew with right sides together using 1/4" seam allowances unless otherwise specified.

Instructions

1. Sew a 1-3/4x8" border strip to one edge of the 6-3/4" character square. Begin sewing 1" from the right edge of the character square and stop at the square's left

edge as shown in Diagram A. Press the seam allowances away from the center.

Diagram A

2. Working in a clockwise direction, add remaining strips to the character square as shown in Diagram B. Complete the bottom seam to finish the front, sewing from the previous stitching to the right edge of the last strip. Press all seam allowances away from the center.

Diagram B

3. From ribbon, cut four 7" lengths and four 13" lengths. Pin the ribbons on the right side of the front, aligning one end of the ribbons with the raw edge of the front. Position two 7" lengths at both the top and bottom corners and two 13" lengths at the left and right corners. Sew the ribbons in place.

4. Fuse the fleece to the wrong side of the backing square following the manufacturer's instructions. With right sides facing, sew the backing to the front, catching the ribbon ends in the stitching and leaving a 3" opening on one edge for turning. Trim the corners and turn right side out. Sew the opening closed.

5. Thread your machine with invisible thread and machine quilt through all layers along the design lines of the preprinted character square and in the ditch along the inner edge of the border.

Pillow Play

Throw them here, throw them there, these pillows can be used everywhere! Choose your favorite block designs or fussy-cut characters from fabric to sew up the pillow patterns on the following pages. These pillows are ideal for the floor, bed, rocker or even the occasional pillow fight.

Materials

Finished size: 14x14"

1/2 yard of animal print fabric for back

1/4 yard of yellow print fabric for front border

1/8 yard of red plaid fabric for front squares

Fabric with motifs to fill 4" front squares

14x14" pillow form

Sew with WRONG sides together using 1/2" seam allowances unless otherwise specified.

Instructions

1. Lay out the 4" squares on a flat surface in 3 rows of 3 squares, alternating the plaid and motif squares in a checkerboard fashion.

2. Sew the squares together in rows, then sew the rows together to complete the pillow front center.

3. Sew a 4x10" yellow print border strip to opposite edges of the front center. Sew a 4x16" yellow border to each of the remaining edges of the pillow front center.

4. To fringe, make 3/8" cuts 1/4" to 3/8" apart along the sewn seams of the pillow front.

5. Sew the pillow front to the back, leaving an 8" opening in the bottom edge.

6. Insert the pillow form into the pillow cover. Use a zipper foot to sew the opening closed, sewing 1/2" from the raw edges. Fringe the outer seam allowances of the pillow cover as in Step 4.

Nine-Patch Chenille Pillow

Cut the Fabric

From animal print, cut:
    1—16" back square

From yellow print, cut:
    2—4x10" border strips
    2—4x16" border strips

From red plaid, cut:
    4—4" front squares

From motif fabric, cut:
    5—4" front squares, centering a motif in each square

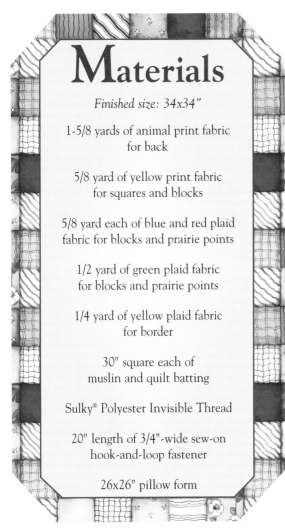

Materials

Finished size: 34x34"

1-5/8 yards of animal print fabric for back

5/8 yard of yellow print fabric for squares and blocks

5/8 yard each of blue and red plaid fabric for blocks and prairie points

1/2 yard of green plaid fabric for blocks and prairie points

1/4 yard of yellow plaid fabric for border

30" square each of muslin and quilt batting

Sulky® Polyester Invisible Thread

20" length of 3/4"-wide sew-on hook-and-loop fastener

26x26" pillow form

Pinwheel Pillow

Sew with right sides together using 1/4" seam allowances unless otherwise specified.

Cut the Fabric

From animal print, cut:
    2—30-1/2x27-1/2" back rectangles

From yellow print, cut:
    4—9" squares
    10—5-1/8" block squares

From blue plaid, cut:
    4—5-1/8" block squares
    8—8" prairie point squares

From green plaid, cut:
    2—5-1/8" block squares
    8—8" prairie point squares

From red plaid, cut:
    4—5-1/8" block squares
    8—8" prairie point squares

From yellow plaid, cut:
    4—1-1/4x44" strips;
    from the strips cut 2—1-1/4x26"
    and 2—1-1/4x27-1/2" border strips

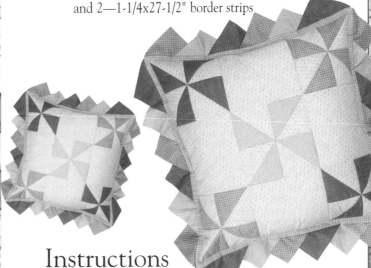

Instructions

Assemble the Pinwheel Blocks

1. With right sides together, layer the 5-1/8" squares in pairs, using a yellow print with each of the plaid squares. Cut the layered squares in half diagonally as shown in Diagram A to make 20 sets of triangles.

Diagram A

2. Sew 1/4" from the diagonal edge of each pair as shown in Diagram B to make a square. Press the seam allowances toward the plaid triangles.

Diagram B

3. Arrange sets of four squares as shown in Diagram C. Sew the squares together in rows and then sew the rows together to make 5 pinwheel blocks.

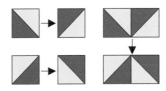

Diagram C

Assemble the Pillow Front

1. Lay out the pinwheel blocks and the 9" yellow print squares in three rows of three blocks, using Diagram D as a guide.

Diagram D

2. Sew the blocks together in rows. Press the seam allowances of each row to one side, alternating the direction with each row.

3. Sew the rows together to complete the pillow front center. Press the seam allowances toward the center row.

4. Sew a 1-1/4x26" yellow plaid border strip to the side edges of the pillow front center. Press the seam allowances toward the border.

5. Sew a 1-1/4x27-1/2" yellow plaid border to the top and bottom edges of the pillow front center. Press the seam allowances toward the border.

Complete the Pillow Cover

1. Smooth out the muslin square on a flat surface and center the batting on the muslin. Center the pillow front, right side up, on the batting. Baste the layers together.

2. Thread your machine with invisible thread and machine quilt in the ditch along all edges of the pinwheel blocks. Trim the batting and muslin even with the raw edge of the pillow front.

3. For the prairie points, refer to Diagram E. Fold each 8" square in half diagonally with wrong sides facing and press. Fold in half again, forming a smaller triangle and press.

Diagram E

4. Pin the prairie points to the right side of the pillow front in the desired color order, aligning the long raw edge of each prairie point with the raw edge of the

pillow front. Begin at a corner, overlapping the points as shown in Diagram F by slipping the folded edge of a prairie point into the open side of the adjacent triangle. Adjust the overlap as needed to fit 6 points on each edge. Sew the points to the pillow front.

Diagram F

5. Fold each of the back rectangles in half with wrong sides facing, aligning the 27-1/2" edges opposite the fold. Press and baste along the raw edges of each back rectangle.

6. Smooth the pillow front on a flat surface. Position a back rectangle on the right half of the pillow front, aligning three edges with the folded edge near the center. Position the second back rectangle over the remaining half of the pillow front in the same manner. Pin, then sew the overlapped areas on the back together at the edges; do not sew to the front at this time.

7. Sew the hook side of the fastener to the wrong side of the upper back piece, centering it along the folded edge. Mark the location for the loop side of the fastener on the right side of the lower back piece and sew the fastener in place.

8. Edge-stitch along the fold of the upper back piece from each end of the fastener to the raw edge as shown in Diagram G.

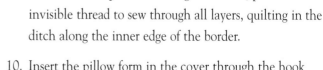

Diagram G

9. With right sides together, sew the pillow front to the back. Turn the pillow cover right side out; press. Use invisible thread to sew through all layers, quilting in the ditch along the inner edge of the border.

10. Insert the pillow form in the cover through the hook and loop fastener opening.

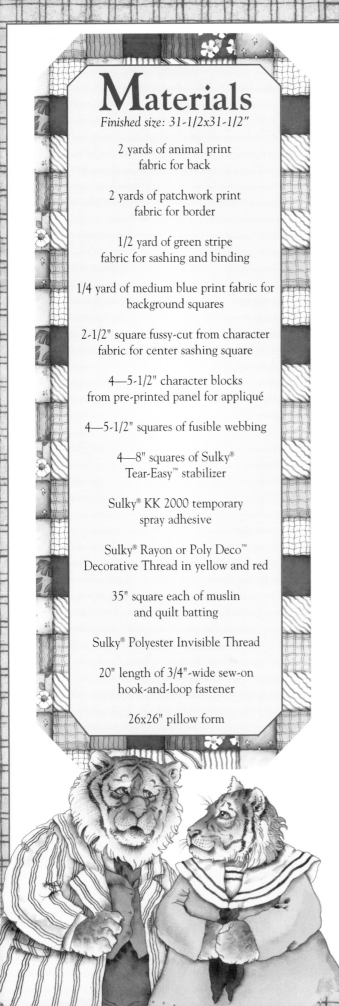

Materials

Finished size: 31-1/2x31-1/2"

2 yards of animal print
fabric for back

2 yards of patchwork print
fabric for border

1/2 yard of green stripe
fabric for sashing and binding

1/4 yard of medium blue print fabric for
background squares

2-1/2" square fussy-cut from character
fabric for center sashing square

4—5-1/2" character blocks
from pre-printed panel for appliqué

4—5-1/2" squares of fusible webbing

4—8" squares of Sulky®
Tear-Easy™ stabilizer

Sulky® KK 2000 temporary
spray adhesive

Sulky® Rayon or Poly Deco™
Decorative Thread in yellow and red

35" square each of muslin
and quilt batting

Sulky® Polyester Invisible Thread

20" length of 3/4"-wide sew-on
hook-and-loop fastener

26x26" pillow form

Panel Pillow
Cut the Fabric

From animal print, cut:
  2—31-1/2x33-1/2" backing rectangles

From patchwork print for border, cut:
  4—6-3/4x35" border strips

From green stripe, cut:
  1—2-1/2x44" strip; from the strip cut
    4—2-1/2x8-3/4" sashing strips
  4—2-3/4x44" binding strips

From medium blue print, cut:
  4—8-3/4" background squares

Instructions

Appliqué the Blocks

1. Fuse a webbing square on the wrong side of each character block, following the manufacturer's instructions. Remove the paper backing. Center and fuse a block on each of the 8-3/4" medium blue print background squares.

2. Center an 8" square of tear-away stabilizer behind the fused block on the back of each background square with temporary spray adhesive. Satin stitch over the edges of the fused block with red decorative thread. For an added touch, use yellow thread to machine buttonhole stitch directly over the satin stitching. Tear away the stabilizer from the back of the background square.

Assemble the Pillow Front Center

1. Lay out the appliquéd blocks, sashing strips and center sashing square on a flat surface, using Diagram A as a guide.

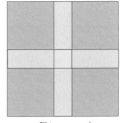

Diagram A

2. To make the block rows, sew together the blocks and sashing strips as indicated in Diagram B. Press all seam allowances one direction.

3. To make the sashing row, sew together the sashing

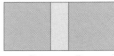

Diagram B

strips and sashing square as indicated in Diagram C. Press all seam allowances the opposite direction from the block rows.

Diagram C

4. Sew the block rows and sashing row together; press.

Assemble the Pillow Front

1. To miter the border, center and pin a 6-3/4x35" patchwork print border strip to one edge of the pillow front. Sew together, beginning and ending the seam 1/4" from the edges of the pillow front as shown in Diagram D. Press the seam allowances toward the border.

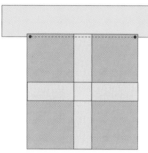

Diagram D

2. Sew the remaining patchwork print border strips to the remaining edges of the pillow center as in Step 1.

3. Working with one corner at a time, draw a diagonal line on the wrong side of the top strip from the corner of the stitching to the point where the two strips meet at the raw edges as shown in Diagram E. Reposition the strips so the bottom border is on top and draw a second line in the same manner.

Diagram E

4. With right sides together, match the drawn lines and pin as shown in Diagram F. Beginning at the inside corner, sew the border strips together directly on the drawn lines. Trim the excess fabric, leaving a 1/4" seam allowance. Press the seam allowances one direction. Repeat Steps 1 to 4 to miter each corner.

Diagram F

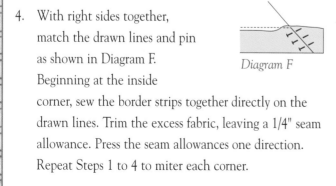

Complete the Pillow Cover

1. Smooth out the muslin square on a flat surface and center the batting on the muslin. Center the pillow front, right side up, on the batting. Baste the layers together.

2. Thread your machine with invisible thread and machine quilt in the ditch along all edges of the appliquéd character blocks, background squares and sashing square. Trim the batting and muslin even with the raw edge of the pillow front.

3. Fold each of the back rectangles in half with wrong sides facing, aligning the 31-1/2" edges opposite the fold. Press and baste along the raw edges of each back rectangle.

4. Smooth the pillow front, right side down, on a flat surface. Position a back rectangle on the bottom half of the pillow front, aligning three edges with the folded edge near the center. Position the second back rectangle over the remaining half of the pillow front in the same manner. Pin, then sew the overlapped areas on the back together at the edges; do not sew to the front at this time.

5. Sew the hook side of the fastener to the wrong side of the upper back piece, centering it along the folded edge. Mark the location for the loop side of the fastener on the right side of the lower back piece and sew the fastener in place.

6. Edge-stitch along the fold of the upper back piece from each end of the fastener to the raw edge as shown in Diagram G.

Diagram G

7. Reposition the back on the front with wrong sides facing and pin together. Sew through all layers 3-1/4" from the raw edges, creating the flange.

8. Sew the short ends of the 2-3/4" wide green stripe binding strips together with diagonal seams to form one long binding strip. Trim the seam allowances to 1/4" and press open. Fold the strip in half lengthwise with wrong sides together; press.

9. Beginning at the center of one edge of the pillow cover, place the binding strip on the right side of the pillow front, aligning the raw edges of the binding with the raw edges of the pillow cover. Fold over the beginning of the binding strip about 1/2". Sew through all layers 1/4" from the raw edges, mitering the corners. Trim away the excess binding, leaving 1/2" at the end to overlap the beginning of the strip.

10. Fold the binding to the back of the pillow to cover the machine stitching; press. Slip stitch the folded edge of the binding in place or sew in the ditch along the binding, catching the folded edge of the binding on the back of the pillow.

11. Insert the pillow form in the cover through the hook-and-loop fastener opening.

Materials

Finished size: 16-1/2x16-1/2"

1 yard of all-over check print fabric for front squares, inner border, outer border and backing

1/8 yard each of blue, green, red and yellow plaid fabrics for front squares and inner border

19" square of quilt batting

14x14" pillow form

Patchwork Pillow
Cut the Fabric

From all-over check, cut:

 2—17x20-1/2" back rectangles

 5—4-1/2" front squares

 2—1-3/4x44" strips; from the strips cut 2—1-3/4x17" and 2—1-3/4x14-1/2" outer border strips

 1—1-1/2x44" strip;
 from the strip cut 4—1-1/2x4-1/2" inner border strips

From each plaid, cut:

 1—4-1/2" front square

 1—1-1/2x5-1/2" inner border strip

 1—1-1/2x4-1/2" inner border strip

Sew with right sides together using 1/4" seam allowances unless otherwise specified.

Instructions

Assemble the Pillow Front

1. Lay out the front squares and the inner border strips on a flat surface, using the photograph on page 45 and Diagram A as guides.

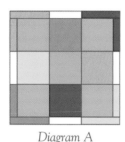

Diagram A

2. To make the inner border rows, sew together the inner border strips as indicated in Diagram B. Press the seam allowances of each row to the left.

Diagram B

3. To make the square/inner border rows, sew together the squares and inner border strips as indicated in Diagram C. Press the seam allowances of the center row to the left and the remaining two rows to the right.

Diagram C

4. Sew the rows together; press.

5. Sew a 1-3/4x14-1/2" outer border strip to the top and bottom edges of the pillow front. Press the seam allowances toward the outer border.

6. Sew a 1-3/4x17" outer border to the left and right edges of the pillow front. Press the seam allowances toward the outer borders.

Complete the Pillow Cover

1. Smooth out the batting square on a flat surface and center the pillow front, right side up, on top of the batting. Baste the layers together.

2. Machine quilt a 2" square centered on each of the front squares and in the ditch along the outer edge of the inner border as shown in Diagram D. Trim the batting even with the raw edges of the pillow front.

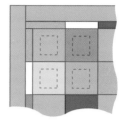

Diagram D

3. Fold each back rectangle in half with wrong sides together, aligning the 17" edges; press.

4. Smooth the pillow front, right side up, on a flat surface. Position a back rectangle on the pillow front, aligning three edges with the folded edge near the center of the pillow front. Position the remaining back rectangle over the remaining half of the pillow front in the same manner. Sew the pillow backs to the pillow front.

5. Turn the pillow cover right side out. Sew 1" from the outer edges of the pillow cover, creating a narrow flange. Insert the pillow form into the pillow cover.

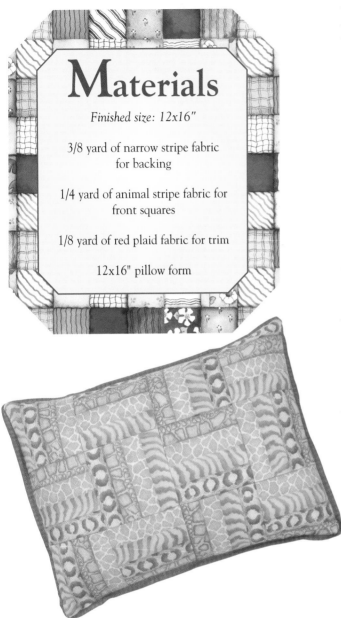

Materials

Finished size: 12x16"

3/8 yard of narrow stripe fabric for backing

1/4 yard of animal stripe fabric for front squares

1/8 yard of red plaid fabric for trim

12x16" pillow form

Animal Stripe Pillow
Cut the Fabric

From narrow stripe, cut:
  1—12-1/2x16-1/2" back rectangle

From animal stripe, cut:
  12—4-1/2" front squares

From red plaid, cut:
  2—1-1/4x44" trim strips

Sew with right sides together using 1/4" seam allowances unless otherwise specified.

Instructions

1. Lay out the 4-1/2" squares on a flat surface in 3 rows of 4 squares, alternating the direction of the stripes as shown in Diagram A and the photograph at left.

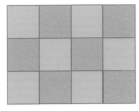

Diagram A

2. Sew the squares together in rows, and then sew the rows together to complete the pillow front.

3. Sew the short ends of the 1-1/4"-wide red plaid trim strips together to form one long binding strip. Press the seam allowances open. Fold the strip in half lengthwise with wrong sides together; press.

4. Beginning at the center of one edge of the pillow front, place the trim strip on the right side, aligning the raw edges of the trim with the raw edges of the pillow front. Begin stitching 1-1/2" from end of trim strip, sewing 1/4" from the raw edges. Stop stitching 1-1/2" from the point where the trim ends meet. Cut one end of trim strip so it overlaps the other end by 1". Fold under 1/2" of overlapping trim and wrap it around the other end as shown in Diagram B; finish stitching.

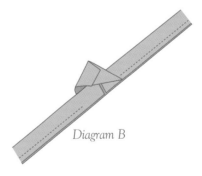

Diagram B

5. Sew the pillow front to the back atop the trim sewing line, leaving an 8" opening in the bottom edge.

6. Turn the pillow cover right side out. Insert the pillow form into the pillow cover. Sew the opening closed.

Stow-It-Away Trunk

A purchased steamer trunk lined with fabric and decorated with travel motifs is a great place to store blankets, stuffed animals or pillows.

◆◆◆◆◆

Materials

Trunk

Yellow print fabric for lining

Pre-printed fussy-cut fabric

Tape measure

Spray adhesive

1/4"-wide red bias tape

Craft glue

Instructions

1. Use a tape measure to find the measurements of each surface on the inside of the trunk that you wish to cover with fabric. Use these measurements to cut the appropriate size from the yellow print fabric.

2. Working with one piece at a time, apply spray adhesive to the wrong side of each fabric piece. Center the fabric piece, adhesive side down, on the coordinating surface of the trunk and smooth from the center out.

3. Cut lengths of bias tape to cover the raw edges of the fabric at the top of the trunk base and at the top and corners of the lid. Glue the bias tape in place.

4. To embellish the trunk, fussy-cut motifs from pre-printed fabric. Spray adhesive onto the wrong side of the motifs and press onto the outside surfaces of the trunk in desired locations.